# EMPOWERED

## HEAR MY WORDS

Edited By Donna Samworth

First published in Great Britain in 2021 by:

Young Writers
Remus House
Coltsfoot Drive
Peterborough
PE2 9BF
Telephone: 01733 890066
Website: www.youngwriters.co.uk

Printed and bound in the UK by BookPrintingUK
Website: www.bookprintinguk.com
YB0489N

# ⋆ FOREWORD ⋆

Since 1991, here at Young Writers we have celebrated the awesome power of creative writing, especially in young adults where it can serve as a vital method of expressing their emotions and views about the world around them. In every poem we see the effort and thought that each student published in this book has put into their work and by creating this anthology we hope to encourage them further with the ultimate goal of sparking a life-long love of writing.

Our latest competition for secondary school students, Empowered, challenged young writers to consider what was important to them. We wanted to give them a voice, the chance to express themselves freely and honestly, something which is so important for these young adults to feel confident and listened to. They could give an opinion, share a memory, consider a dilemma, impart advice or simply write about something they love. There were no restrictions on style or subject so you will find an anthology brimming with a variety of poetic styles and topics. We hope you find it as absorbing as we have.

We encourage young writers to express themselves and address subjects that matter to them, which sometimes means writing about sensitive or contentious topics. If you have been affected by any issues raised in this book, details on where to find help can be found at www.youngwriters.co.uk/info/other/contact-lines

# ✭ CONTENTS ✭

Esther Lang (15)                          73

## John O'Gaunt School, Hungerford

Emily Aldridge (15)                       74
Naomi Fox-Shatford                        77
Abriana McDonald (16)                     78
Amy Muscroft (16)                         80
Bebe Thatcher (15)                        82
Katie Griffiths (15)                      84
Victoria Jaworska (16)                    86
Miles Morris (15)                         88
Lewi Kyle-Jacobs                          90
Madison Stephens (15)                     91
Rebekah Standen (15)                      92
Ben Brown                                 93
Helen Gray (16)                           94
Max Wheeler (16)                          95
Enzo Scarlett (15)                        96
Archie Boswell-Pendleton (15)            97
Maude Williams                            98

## King James' School, Almondbury

Loretta Clements (13)                     99
Eoin Morris (13)                         100
Lilli Walsh (14)                         102
Imogen Welsh (13)                        104
Lola Harber (14)                         106
Chloe Taylor (13)                        108
Isla Farnsworth (14)                     109
Brooke Carroll (13)                      110
Hanan Lateef (13)                        111
Kiana Beckley (13)                       112
Costya Whitehouse (13)                   113
Sam Fawcett (13)                         114
Eva Henman (13)                          115
Evie Taylor (13)                         116
Georgia Lynch (13)                       117
Katie Shaw (13)                          118

## Loreto Grammar, Altrincham

Charlotte Reddington (12)                119
Christelle Bitar (12)                    120
Sophie Popplewell (12)                   122
Eloho Arorote (12)                       124
Abigail Bailey (12)                      126
Isabella Burton (12)                     127
Molly Kilburn (12)                       128
Alys Price-Jones (12)                    130
Alexandra Higginson (12)                 131
Amy Yates (13)                           132
Cara Gregory (12)                        133
Elizabeth Stansfield (13)                134

## Maesteg Comprehensive School, Maesteg

Kian Searle (12)                         135
Tristian Bowen (12)                      136
Grace Finnemore (12)                     137
Daisy Purnell (12)                       138
Linkon Edwards (12)                      139
Rhys Thomas (13)                         140
Thomas Huggins (12)                      141
Kyle Sparrow (12)                        142
Logan Jones (12)                         143

## NWKAPS - The Rosemary Centre, Gravesend

Joshua Ogabi (15)                        144
Holly McAllister (15)                    145
Riannha Samuel (15)                      146

## Ryde School With Upper Chine, Ryde

Emma Boddington (14)                     147
Alice Owen (14)                          148
Caitlin Dologhan (14)                    150
Jessica Holt (14)                        151
Catherine Brading-Palmer (14)            152
Cully Trevallion (14)                    153
Ella Brear (14)                          154

Sophie Corry (15)                   155
Finley Boxall (15)                  156
Wilona Rong (14)                    157
Alice Holyoake (14)                 158
Aashima Maheshwari (14)             159
Kai Miller (14)                     160
Lucie Dartigues (14)                161

## Sir John Leman High School, Beccles

Evie Ellis (11)                     162
Daniel Peckham (12)                 163
Samuel Thompson (11)                164
Stephanie Roe (11)                  165
Benjamin Renicar (12)               166
Xavi Lee (11)                       167
Hunter Renicar (12)                 168
Eden Benson-Smith (11)              169
Kaila Smith (11)                    170
Harry Thompson (11)                 171

## St Ronan's College, Lurgan

Jamie Scullion (12)                 172
Mia McDowell (15)                   173
Enda Scullion (15)                  174
David Konon (12)                    175
Ariana Pereira De Jesus (14)        176
Ellie Towe (14)                     177
Kaitlyn Farrell (14)                178
Aliyah Armstrong (13)               179
Ava-Rose Keenan (15)                180
Brea Lavery (13)                    181
Ruairi Campbell (15)                182
Emma Mallon (13)                    183
Sade Armstrong (14)                 184
Dylan Jennings (13)                 185
Connor Quinn (12)                   186
Olivia Crosby (13)                  187
Beth Cushnahan (14)                 188
Caoimhe Hatchell (14)               189

# THE POEMS

# Listen

Listen

Words go to the left
And go to the right of them
The future is beyond the unseeable
But incompetence blinds them

Listen!

Words still go to the left
And still go to the right of them
The future is still beyond and unreachable
Arrogance still binds them

Hey, listen

For your thousandth endless fervour
The changes you speak of sound impactful
But all I see are little voices diminished
Must we implore them on our knees?

Listen
Listen
Hey, listen!

## Christopher Ting (17)
Abbey College, Cambridge

# Cut Flower

Ten years of living as an ugly sunflower:
I pulled on the dress Mom bought.
Looking in the mirror with half an eye,
I couldn't see the way it was exposing my graceless body,
Fat arms, fat legs, unflattering skin
I couldn't see it all, I couldn't!
Shivering at the sight of people talking, no?
I didn't care, I didn't!
Fat and plain, not as ravishing as her mother.
Small eyes, dark skin, not as lovely as her sister.

Thirteen years of living as an ugly sunflower:
I pulled on the dress Mom bought.
Then I took it off. People would look, people would talk.
Oversized tee, black leggings. There, I didn't look as fat now.
Isn't that her sister? Wow, much clever and brighter.
Eyes down, mouth shut. I wouldn't sound so stupid now.
Damp pillows, wide eyes - I couldn't bring myself to sleep.
A lone sunflower in the midst of beautiful ones.
A blot on the landscape.

Sixteen years of living as an ugly sunflower:
Slow, fat, dumb, ugly and plain.
I pulled on the clothes I bought.
No, this was all wrong. I looked hideous.

What would my friends say if they saw me like this?
What would the adults say?
Fat people don't wear crop tops.
How come the ten-year-old me never knew, never noticed
Never cared?

Sunflowers - they grow towards the sun,
While I keep my head to the ground.
Gardeners cut the blooming sunflowers
They cut flowers because flowers are beautiful.
I cut myself because I look bad.
And insecure and worthless.

## Phuong Nguyen Dang (17)
Abbey College, Cambridge

# Society Said

The amount of pressure society puts on women is insane

In order to look pretty
They must go through pain.
Legs should be clean with no visible hair,
Society treats those quite unfair.
Social media, magazines, newspapers, TVs,
Force expectations
And standards to reach.

You must wear more make-up,
Satisfy male gaze,
This way you will never
Fail to get more praise.
But don't try too hard
And don't wear too much.
Men sense desperation
Please don't be seen as such.

Boys say that they like very natural girls
No extra extensions, big eyes like pearls.
Your lips should be the bright colour red,
'The colour of passion', society said.
Don't show too much skin,
You don't want to be shamed,
And as a result, degraded and named.

This forced prematurity,
Will cause insecurity.
It affects body image,
Health and mentality,
Yet this is our life and this is reality.

The amount of self-hate this caused is unreal
Our hearts are not being made of steel.
We females can be soft, loving, nurturing creatures.
Without having all of the sexy features.
We can be strong, independent, determined,
Above all athletic,
Without the need to use artificial cosmetic
We females are beautiful, authentic, empowered.

Society doesn't need to be such a coward.

## Dalial Mutallapova (17)
Abbey College, Cambridge

# Overload

We're all just zeroes or ones
All just Xs or Ys
All just part of the motherboard
All just pixels on a computer
Overload

From creator, to uncredited
From function to forgotten
Overload

Could it have just been an error?
Syntax error?
Logic error?
Human error?
Overload

What is wrong with the code?
Is the one not meant to be there?
Is it just 0s?
Overload

Will the hardware work without software?
Will the 0s work without the 1s?
Will the algorithm work without the function?
Overload

Was this rigged from the start?
Should we reboot?
Overload

Did they copy it
And erase the original?
Overload

Was there ever any rights on it?
Were they usurped?
Overload

Repeat
When 0+1
End loop.

## Gadea De Torres (15)
Abbey College, Cambridge

# The Self-Created World

A bird stands on its tiptoes
Peacefully, powerfully
The moment it flies

Time is muted, reality is frozen
Its feathers turn into fleeting smoke
The firmament is spirituality

The self-created world.

**Yujie Yang (18)**
Abbey College, Cambridge

# It's Just Our Rights

We can be ourselves believe it or not,
We don't care what others think.
Every single one of us is different from the lot,
Even though we are different we still have a link.

"She's gay, that's disgusting,"
So is your attitude.
All of us can be trusting,
I can't believe that it's so rude.

Some of us like boys,
Some of us like girls.
Some of us like both,
Some of us like none.

Some of us identify as a girl,
Others as boys.
Some don't know or can't figure it out yet,
Yet some feel different all the time.

You are you,
I am me.
We wouldn't change ourselves for the world.
People are cruel, selfish and mean,
But you and I,
Me and you,
Can pull this together and argue this through.

## Amelia Rosser (11)
Croesyceiliog School, Croesyceiliog

# The Sausage Dog Of Death

He's 9 foot 2, with icy eyes of blue,
he's so much taller than all of you.

A long dark cloak, and no facial features,
he decides the fate of all earthly creatures.

His name is Death! He'll take your soul!
You're on the list, the bell will toll!

He appears to float beneath his cape,
he'll find you on your sell-by date.

No one can run, and no one hides,
he picks his victims with his scythes.*

*He has multiple scythes now instead of just one,
due to the COVID pandemic which has ruined the fun.

New COVID rules he follows from Heaven and Hell,
he wears a face mask and carries alcohol gel.

He's had to adapt his reaping methods this time,
because now everyone walks in a one-way line.

But there is one thing that nobody knows,
a little dog follows wherever he goes.

She's black and tan, with short stumpy legs,
her favourite treat is two scrambled eggs.

A tiny sausage dog, she's a Dachshund pup,
she'll lick your face when your time is up.

Her name is Margo! She's so joyful and sweet,
she'll most certainly be the last dog you meet.

Death loves his pet, and she loves her keeper,
the tag on her collar reads: 'If found, return to
Mr G. Reaper.'

She loves days at the beach, and walks in the park,
but stalks Death's victims like a wolf in the dark.

His harvest he gathers, and signs off with blood,
and Margo scoffs dog treats whilst rolling in mud.

He'll stop at nothing you know, *and ye shall be stricken!*
Unless Margo needs a pee or some tasty chicken.

So if you ever see Grim carrying his scythe for a chop,
you'd better be close to a Pets at Home shop.

## Immi Evans (11)
Croesyceiliog School, Croesyceiliog

# Social Media Is Fake

Social media makes you think,
My teeth aren't straight enough and my waist size should shrink,
None of that is true, not one single word,
The models are all edited and the pictures have been blurred.

Social media drill into your brain,
You should look like this, even if it brings you mental pain,
For decades nobody realised how wrong this is,
Spending your time doing a 'How attractive am I?' quiz.

Social media can convince you,
Your nose is too big, though you never thought that was true,
You're perfect as you are, don't dare change a thing,
Although I know the insults always sting.

Social media is fake, don't believe everything on your screen,
You are beautiful and that is something I truly mean.

## Lily Payne (14)
Croesyceiliog School, Croesyceiliog

# What Is The Future Going To Hold For Us?

I wonder what will happen in the future
With all the problems that is happening right now across the world
It is like we are all trapped in one big container
Our voices all need to be heard otherwise it will just be too late.

With all the conflict that is going on around the world right now
We all have to fight to stay safe and survive
We all need to be alert on what is happening at this current time
We all need to look after each other and be kind.

I wonder what the future brings
Whether it will be good or bad
My hope is that the world comes back together and brings us all beautiful things
We shall all love each other.

Please may this come true
Let's hope that the sky comes back blue.

## Jessica George (13)
Croesyceiliog School, Croesyceiliog

# Nightmares

There are nights where I'd lie in bed,
With horrible thoughts going through my head,
Stories brought back from the past,
As they whoosh through my head so fast.

Ghosts and clowns, what could be worse?
Surely, just surely I might be cursed,
As I think about the day ahead,
School and work, what a dread.

Strange images appear in my mind,
In my dreams I wish I were blind,
Thousands of spiders coming from all directions,
They are definitely coming for me, no objections.

I hope one night, I will be asleep,
No more nightmares, not even counting sheep,
Peace and quiet at last,
Not a single noise, and no flashbacks from the past.

## Carys Croke (13)
Croesyceiliog School, Croesyceiliog

# Climate Change

Climate change is changing
The world as we know it is changing fast,
We do know it's changing as it's starting to show,
We need to do something before it grows.

Climate change is in the world
Happening everywhere that we know
We can do something, just do it so
We can live for generations with snow

So please help the planet live, not die
Do it for life so the planet doesn't cry
Otherwise we will have to say goodbye
Think of the planet as a friend, not a foe

Get the planet to live with a happy glow
Change the planet's climate change to slow
Oh, it's time for me to leave
Think of what I have said.

## Laila Judge (11)
Croesyceiliog School, Croesyceiliog

# To Yearn

Reached for a rose,
The sun made it gleam,
Tended its petals,
Only a dream.

Found once a library
Of many desires.
Gave some hope,
Now a possessor.
Fantasy at its peak.

A world of people,
All there for me.
Showing endearment,
But only a longing.

Once reached for a rose,
Got stung by a bee.
Its thorns a barricade
From tending a dream.
A dream that could never be.

Once a library
Of many desires.
Now a room
Of unrealised fantasy.

Badly justified,
A world not to be.
A prayer with no reason,
And no reason to prayer
Is it terrible
To yearn?

## George Tavener (11)
Croesyceiliog School, Croesyceiliog

# Seasons In The Meadow

Alone in the meadow, the air is sweet,
The sky is bright, the flowers are blooming.
Lying in the meadow, the grass a treat,
The scent so pure, the river is flowing.
Running in the meadow, the path unclear,
The branches are swaying, fresh is the breeze.
Rest in the meadow, the bees are all I hear,
Loud, chirping birds call out from the lush trees.
Ablaze in the meadow, colours are changing,
Conkers collected, the acorns are found.
Death in meadow, the wind is chilling,
Bare trees bring a tear, leaves fall to the ground.
Away from the meadow, my heart is lost,
The ground lacks colour, the winter brings frost.

## Fearne Spear (13)
Croesyceiliog School, Croesyceiliog

# Equality

We're all humans, we're all the same species
So why treat each other differently
So why are we still being big bullies
So why can't we all just live contently?

Racism is one of the biggest problems
Black Lives Matter is a massive subject
We are splitting people into columns
Treating them as if they are just objects

Why people do this I don't have a clue
We are being cruel to kind humans
Just because they don't look the same as you
You start spreading lies and lots of rumours

Please can we treat everyone equally
So we can all live nice and peacefully?

**Ruby Bailey (13)**
Croesyceiliog School, Croesyceiliog

# Sticks

A stereotypical stick, tall and thin
It holds no organs, it doesn't even read
It's not human, the stick isn't our twin
Does not even have blood, can't sign a deed
I may ramble and ramble but the point
The point is, you don't have to be like sticks
To fit society, you're not disjoined
Social media really did give kicks
It ruined our perception of ourselves
We tried having impossible figures
They also really did ruin themselves
Made themselves have a look of disfigured
Modern media has betrayed us all
It meant to raise us but brought us a fall.

**Elizabeth Jacobs (13)**
Croesyceiliog School, Croesyceiliog

# In The Woods

In the wild wind,
In the woods they live,
You can ask them a question,
But they'll never give.

When I was little,
I travelled afar,
To have a little peep
Of what was inside that jar.

I found coins upon coins
Made of nothing else but gold,
I picked up one, my hand burnt badly,
Then time went on quickly, and it all began to go old.

A boy down the street
Decided to do the same,
Then he went missing,
And there was no one to blame.

Now we all learned
Not to go near
The house of madness, sadness, and fear.

**Daniel Harris (11)**
Croesyceiliog School, Croesyceiliog

# No Matter

No matter who you are, we all have an image.
We look at our image differently to others around us,
We pick out the insecurities, the likes, dislikes.
But your image is yours to love, to show off
And feel proud of the skin you were born in.
You shouldn't need to change yourself
Because your nose or ears are bigger or smaller than others.
What matters is that you take care of your image,
Smile and feel proud because you should.
Embrace the skin you're in, love it, care for it.
That's all that matters, not what people say or how others look.

## Grace Axford (14)

Croesyceiliog School, Croesyceiliog

# My Monster Bert

Bert is a monster who lives under my bed,
He's fluffy and blue with two yellow horns on his head.

With stumpy little hands and bright yellow eyes,
Whenever I see him I get a surprise.

Bert is monster who is fluffy and short,
He chews on my shoes and always gets caught.

With little purple feet and glasses to see,
Bert is so friendly to me.

Bert is my friend, we play through the night,
He's got four little teeth, but he does not bite.

With cuddly fur so soft to the touch,
Bert is my friend, I love him so much.

**Finley Jameson-Crook (11)**
Croesyceiliog School, Croesyceiliog

# Between The Bars

Trapped in the darkness alone at night,
Realising no one would ever write,
Peering through these empty bars,
Watching as each guard passes by.

Lost in a room full of unknown faces,
Breaking, stuttering, shaking,
Trapped up, all alone,
Can't cope with the pain anymore.

They took away my freedom,
They took away my pride,
They took away my happiness,
Nothing's left inside.

Never-ending nightmare,
Feel like giving up,
It's difficult,
I've really had enough,
I wish I could escape.

## Renée Wang (11)
Croesyceiliog School, Croesyceiliog

# The Moon

The moon has a face like the clock in the hall
She shines on thieves on the garden wall
On streets and fields and harbour quays
And birdies asleep in the forks of the trees.

The squalling cat and the squeaking mouse,
The bowling dog by the door of the house
The bat that lives in the bed at home
All love to be out by the light of the moon
But all of the things that belong to the day
Cuddle to sleep to be out of her way
And flowers and children close their eyes
Till up in the morning the sun shall rise.

## Chloe Oates
Croesyceiliog School, Croesyceiliog

# About My Identity

**I** nterested in sports but mostly football and really good at it in my opinion, I do also like golf but I'm not as good at it.

**D** oing lots with my life and having fun.

**E** ager to learn and develop to learn more about different subjects.

**N** ice to people at all times.

**T** reat people the way I would like to be treated.

**I** would like to know more about all aspects of my life.

**T** o have people to have a good life like me and to have fun.

**Y** ou all to be treated like each other.

## Oscar Jones (11)

Croesyceiliog School, Croesyceiliog

# Let's All Join The Queue

Line up, get in the queue,
That's what Britain tends to do

All because the media say
Shortages are on the way.

Empty cars that need the fuel,
Because we need to get to school

But the answers are clear to see
Times have changed for you and me

In the past they had to walk
In the morning, time to talk

Now we rush from place to place,
With a mask that covers our face

Perhaps the answer is plain to see
Time to switch off our TVs.

**Jake Washer (12)**
Croesyceiliog School, Croesyceiliog

# Gaming

I immerse myself into the world of gaming.
I transport to a world of pixels and blocks or try to win a game with a little luck.
I spend time designing and building like an architect, solving problems and becoming the best.
I play with my friends and work as a team, win, lose or draw, we'll just go again.
There are no limits to my creativity, whether it's building an island or creating a river, the possibilities are endless.
I often lose track of time and ask, "Just five more minutes."

**Evan Edwards (11)**
Croesyceiliog School, Croesyceiliog

# A Small Shrew

A small shrew scutters through the forest.
The leaves crumple at every step.
A small shrew lives in the ground.
It hears the footsteps in the whole forest.

A small shrew survives through the darkest nights.
Burying in the deepest field.
A small shrew hears the machines roar through the night.
The workers pass as if he isn't there.

A small shrew fights for his forest.
But it is never triumphant.
A small shrew dies for his forest.
Never to be seen again.

**Rory Pritchard (11)**
Croesyceiliog School, Croesyceiliog

# I Love To Game

I love to game,
But unfortunately I have terrible aim.
I enjoy playing online,
Because that's where I can really shine.

I'm always conscious of my time,
Because sitting in a chair can really hurt my spine.
I stopped using my joypad,
It just kept getting me mad.

So now I use a mouse and keyboard,
I'm now clapping bots with a virtual sword.
So now I won a tournament, 300 pounds to my name,
Just kidding, I wish, I'm just really lame.

## Rhys Hobby (13)
Croesyceiliog School, Croesyceiliog

# Environment Safety

The environment is in need of help,
It's changing for the worse,
The animals are in need in the Alps,
The ice is starting to disperse.

Red pandas, snow leopards, tigers,
All going away, forever extinct,
We should all start becoming bikers,
The different habitats have become distinct.

So let's be better and work hard together,
To save our planet and its wonders,
To stop the global warming weather,
And bring an end to the blunders.

## Grace Spencer (14)
Croesyceiliog School, Croesyceiliog

# Flanders' Field

In Flanders' Field
The poppies grow,
Along the grass,
Row in row.

The soldiers put their life on the line,
They hid in trenches trying to survive,
To protect the freedoms that are mine,
Not knowing what the future could hold.

For our future they gave their past,
For our breath,
They gave their last,
Our soldiers gave their lives.

We will remember
Every November,
They gave their lives
And did not surrender.

## Ellie-Grace Piddington (11)
Croesyceiliog School, Croesyceiliog

# Friendship

**F** riends are the family we choose.
**R** eliable and always have your back.
**I** 'll be there when you're happy or sad.
**E** xcited for our future.
**N** icest person you would ever meet
**D** on't ever leave each other behind.
**S** haring worries and dreams.
**H** ilarious and always having fun.
**I** nvolving each other in everything we do.
**P** eople who remember you throughout the years.

## Lexi Hill (11)
Croesyceiliog School, Croesyceiliog

# Save Our World

Our world is burning to the ground
The atmosphere is being destroyed
Our homes will soon be drowned
And it's making the people annoyed

It's up to us to help it survive
Because we only have one world
So don't ruin the hives
And destroy our dream world

The indigenous animals
Red panda, white rhinos
Our beloved carnivores
Will end up like the dinos.

**Sian Fowler (13)**
Croesyceiliog School, Croesyceiliog

# The Environment Of The World

Lots of things are going wrong,
The environment is dying,
And wars are coming too,
We've got to act fast.

Climate change is killing animals,
Polar bears, penguins,
There's no place to live,
We've got to act fast.

Black Lives Matter is getting worse,
From racist people,
Accusing them for no reason,
We've got to act fast.

**Morgan Plow (11)**
Croesyceiliog School, Croesyceiliog

# My Dreams

**M** y dreams can come true if I believe they can
**Y** ou can only try to be your brilliant best

**D** azing into space, dreaming what I want to be
**R** emembering to believe in myself
**E** ach day is the next step to my dreams
**A** chievement is a must to succeed
**M** aking the most of life
**S** tepping stones are the keys to my future.

## Charlie Walker (12)
Croesyceiliog School, Croesyceiliog

# The World Is Dying

The world is dying, because of us.
Temperatures rising. The air filled with dust.
A greenhouse effect in the atmosphere.
If we don't change, the end will be near.
There's litter in the ocean and all over the floor,
But we don't stop; we just litter more.
It all must end now, we must change our ways,
But to reverse the damage, it all seems a haze.

**Elliott Birchley (11)**
Croesyceiliog School, Croesyceiliog

# Holidays

**H** olidays mean happiness
**O** ld buckets and spades tossed into the boot
**L** ong journeys full of anticipation
**I** spy to pass the time
**D** ays spent playing in the deep blue sea
**A** beach full of laughing children
**Y** achts bobbing in the harbour as we stroll by at night
**S** un going down on another perfect day.

## Sophie Davies (11)

Croesyceiliog School, Croesyceiliog

# CR7

You're dedicated and disciplined, your fitness is the best
Your speed, aim and skill make you better than the rest
It's clear you are gifted, jumping up to 3m high
I aspire to be just like you, the limit is the sky
You do so much for charity but for that you never gloat
674 goals, 229 assists, that's why, CR7, you're the GOAT.

**Tyler Ryan (11)**
Croesyceiliog School, Croesyceiliog

# Autumn

**A** ll in coats as the stormy weather approaches the town
**U** mbrellas shoot up as the rain pours down
**T** he leaves transform colours of copper, golden and red
**U** nder the comfort of their home people snuggle in bed
**M** any more hours of darkness descends
**N** othing's as fun as hot chocolate with friends.

## Mia Worsfold (11)

Croesyceiliog School, Croesyceiliog

# Our Planet

**O** ur planet is beautiful

**U** nique in every way

**R** ecycle and reuse

**P** lease help look after and care for our planet

**L** ove and care for it

**A** dore and love it

**N** ever stop caring because

**E** arth is so interesting and special but

**T** ime is running out.

## Jessica Berry (11)
Croesyceiliog School, Croesyceiliog

# The Eyes

I sit, I stare, this isn't fair
They follow me, the eyes
There on the floor, there on the wall
I can't escape, they're everywhere!
They block my comfort, they make me scared
I wanna hide, but they don't seem to care.
My eyes go blurry, I don't see eyes
All I see is people saying hi.

## Janna Farkas (11)
Croesyceiliog School, Croesyceiliog

# Wonderful Creatures

**P** uppies' smiles are full of glee.
**U** nconditional love makes them lovely.
**P** uppies are small.
**P** uppies love us all!
**I** nnocent puppies shouldn't get hurt anymore.
**E** ven if they don't look scary at all.
**S** top hurting puppies and love them all!

## Madeleine Freebury (11)

Croesyceiliog School, Croesyceiliog

# Point Of View

Things are changing in the world
The waters are rising due to climate change
That no one is doing anything about it
This makes me nervous
One day this planet will be covered in water
But as a planet we have a chance
To make things right
A chance that won't be there in the future.

## Isabelle Jackson (12)
Croesyceiliog School, Croesyceiliog

# Sky

Sky is blue
And we can have hair like it too
We like the sky because it tells you if it is day or night
And as well when it is at night watch out because you might
get a fright
So that is why you should appreciate the sky
Or you might go up very high.

## Charlie Mitchell (11)
Croesyceiliog School, Croesyceiliog

# The World Of Ronaldo

**R** eally amazing at football
**O** n schedule every day
**N** ever putting his head down
**A** lways trying his best
**L** ike never relying on teammates
**D** etermined
**O** n it like a car bonnet.

## Tristan Slade (11)
Croesyceiliog School, Croesyceiliog

# Recycle

Recycle everything we can
Everyone can play a part
Cans and tins, glass bottles too
Yoghurt pots and food
Cereal boxes and bottles of milk
Let's work together to save our
Earth!

**Sam Thomas (12)**
Croesyceiliog School, Croesyceiliog

# My Horse

How I love my little lovely horse,
I will brush him very well, of course
I will comb his tail and much more
I will take him out every day
Because he likes to be adored.

## Seren Jeffries (11)
Croesyceiliog School, Croesyceiliog

# Time Is Running Out

Life is complicated
There will always be problems
Stress is just a distraction
Think of what is more important
Doing what you believe is right.

## Brooke Fairclough (12)
Croesyceiliog School, Croesyceiliog

# Vanity

I study wrinkles on white thighs when I prod them
Like ripples in jam coming to boil, in ponds I dip my fingers
in,
Aftershocks of a touch.

Hair, roaming from my centre, reminding me
Of the reaching branches of a tree
Or veins of a city.

Golden eyes that seem
To change with the seasons
And appear somewhat alien.

Locks that caress the undulations of my spine
Like seaweed washed up, a voyager
On a temporary stay -

Don't run your fingers through it, I laugh,
She's like a venus flytrap,
Once she has you she won't let you go.

Fingers, my fingers, the same chewed fingernails
That scratched the striped pelt of a tiger,
Felt the freshly dipped orange strands fall through my
fingertips

Believe me when I say I was never meant
For the ordinary but the extraordinary
Which always seemed to happen upon me

By chance, bumped into me, coming or going
And paused as if to say:
"Ah, I've been looking for you."

Arms that wrestled with over half a ton of muscle
In a bizarre language of heels
I learned to keep down for most of my childhood.

Skin, like I've been peppered with meteor atoms
I imagine little rovers explore
But smooth, soft,

Sprinkled with a sepia dust that leaves me two-toned,
Spotted like the Dalmatians and Appaloosas
The child in me adored

And that's only the exterior, I haven't yet
Gifted you a tour of the inside of me.
The most futuristic technology behind my mechanisms

The synapses and neurons that create
This happy chaos of my home,
Always heading for the stars

When space is in us;
My apparatus built by the atoms of suns
That died so I could be born.

So how could you ask me to find any imperfection
When stardust of supernovas
Painted this?

There's no one I'd rather be than me
No body I'd rather be in than my own
My head is my favourite place to be

And you won't find me apologising for it.

**Brooke Cameron (17)**
Dalriada School, Ballymoney

# I Love The Penguins

I love the penguins with their short-barrelled chests
And the long-drawn-out orange beaks they wear.
The daddies are sublime, holding the chick eggs
Whilst the long, frigid Antarctic winter goes on.

Adorable the chicks are, with their fuzzy down feathers
When they are born,
Growing up into hens and cocks, the colours morph
Into shades of jet-black and snowy white.

I love the penguins, as they nosedive
Into the cavernous, midnight-blue ocean,
To seize silvery lanternfish and sprats.
They waddle with their webbed feet in a back-and-forth manner
Like old men shuffling for the bus.

Swimming rapidly, they evade the enormous sharks
With their ready-to-stab teeth.
The penguins blissfully lift up their flippers
Like quiet doves in the night sky.

**Harry Johnston (11)**
Dalriada School, Ballymoney

# The Power Of Words

There are many weapons in today's world,
Of which you've probably heard.
Some are sharp and strong, some are dull and weak,
But none of them are like the word.

The word can bring people together,
Or split relationships apart.
The word can confess a truth, a feeling,
Or break a person's heart.

In this day and age, words are vital,
To make a point, take a stand or be heard.
But some people are forced to keep them inside,
A fact that I find appalling and absurd,
That they can't display the power of their words.

They could have been the voice of change,
The one who fixed unfair laws.
But their governments simply don't listen to them,
And maintain their biased flaws.

In a world already with numerous issues,
With more and more every day.
People like them, voices like theirs,
Can make their country's problems go away.

Their words may not have a physical form,
But are stronger than any sword can be.

They can be used to give others a voice,
Or create racial and sexual equality.

Whether you're protesting in the streets,
Or talking to your friends and classmates.
Ensure your words are nice and friendly and kind,
Or the resulting effects won't be so great,
For this is a message that can't be deferred,
Always be careful with your every word.

## Jack McIlrath (15)
Dalriada School, Ballymoney

# Our Earth

By 2050, there will be more plastic in the ocean than fish in
the sea
How does that make you feel?
If you don't care, you might as well stop reading now
You still here?
We need to realise the problem, not discard it like rubbish
This needs to change now!
If you think someone else will do something, what if they
don't?
You can make a difference!
If more people do that, we can change for the better.

Small changes, small things we do have a big effect
If we raise awareness of the problem, we can all work
together
Just look at Greta Thunberg
She has changed our Earth
You can do that too!

Earth is 4.5 billion years old
Us, 140 thousand years old
If you condensed the Earth's lifespan into 24 hours
We have been on this planet for three seconds
Look what we have done in three seconds!

At a record pace we have increased the extinction of
animals
By 1000 times the normal rate
In the next 10 to 100 years, every animal we love is
predicted to be extinct
Tiger gone
Elephant gone
Gorilla gone
In three seconds
It is our duty to protect Mother Nature
Together, as one.

**Fergus Glenn (12)**
Dalriada School, Ballymoney

# Why?

Why?
The question repeats itself in my head,
As I try to settle down for bed.
Why do people hurt others?
I disappear under the covers,
But the query still haunts me,
Drowning out all the other thoughts, you see?
Why? Why do we litter?
The little voice in my head continues to chitter.
Why? Why do we cause creatures pain?
The question turns me insane.
Why? Why do we destroy our home?
My mind begins to roam.
"Stop! Stop!" I cry
And I sit up and begin to sigh.
"I'll fix all the mistakes!"
"No matter what it takes!"
I imagine it and whisper under my breath,
Into the cold midnight air, crawling like death
"Yes... but I need help!"

## Ciara Watson (12)
Dalriada School, Ballymoney

58

# Eyelash

One day I lost an eyelash
I made a wish and blew
It made its journey across the sea
And through the tangled wood
It's very rare for an eyelash
To complete the journey
Lots of them have failed
And fluttered down to the surface
But this one is special
It got through the wood
And landed in the factory
Where all wishes come true
The factory took the eyelash
And granted that one wish
And sent it with the eyelash
To make that wish come true
Now if you see an eyelash
Gliding in the wind
Make a wish and maybe
It will grant that wish!

## Abigail Goudie (11)
Dalriada School, Ballymoney

# Forgotten

Depressing and empty locked shop
Empty tabletop

*Sorry We Are Closed* sign on the door
Dusty clothes inside that once were worn

Closing-down sale, going fast
Originality lost in the past

Online shopping on the rise
While local businesses shrink in size

Mass production is all you see
"Buy one now! Get two free!"

Generic outlets fill the streets
Small businesses surrender to defeat.

**Gracie Rose McKeever (11)**
Dalriada School, Ballymoney

# Choices

Words are free; you can choose
They can create, they can illustrate such pleasure
They can encourage, they can be helpful
Words can destroy, cause deep depression
Words can hurt, they can harm, humiliate
Or even make you lose a mate
Words are strong and they can be long
It's time for you to make a choice
And use your voice!

**Georgia Dougherty (13)**
Dalriada School, Ballymoney

# Sorry To The Future Generations

Sorry to the future generations.
Sorry you couldn't see the things that we saw
Sorry for the things that we've done
Sorry for not thinking about you.
Sorry for ignoring the future and only thinking about the present.
Sorry for taking things from you
Things that mattered to you
Things that were special to you
Things that are magical to you.
But they are gone, extinct, taken away, perished.
But you know what that is, the problem, instead of perishing things we should
cherish them
Instead of hating we should try loving
Instead of fighting we should just unite
Instead of pushing let us just hold on to each other
Let us hold on to our friends, our family, our loved ones and even strangers
Because you know what? It's just rude to be this cruel to our planet.
Why do not we try to solve the problems instead of just talking about them?

Why ignore and try to feel good instead of just fixing the problem and feeling
good.
Feeling good about what we did.
Feeling good about who we are.
Feeling good about what we'll be remembered for?
So, let's stop saying 'sorry' and let's start saying
You know what? This is just too rude to be this cruel to our planet
Let's start helping it, let's start lifting it up again,
Let's be united
Let's not be rude to our planet but thankful.
Let's just be something we are all proud of.

## Max Law
Dollar Academy, Dollar

# To The Class Of 2026...

We had English
we had maths
that we didn't all enjoy
but here we are
those equations are no use
x isn't going to help me in an interview
neither is Shakespeare
to be helpful or not to be helpful...? That is the question
but here we are.

We had politics,
we had languages
that we didn't all enjoy
but here we are
Donald Trump is an idiot
his arguments won't get me anywhere
neither will bonjour
je fais la vaisselle
doing the dishes won't help me
but here we are.

We had drama
we had art
that we didn't all enjoy
but here we are
freeze frame is no use

who needs that acting mask?
Paint is no use either,
paint can't always cover up my mistakes
but here we are.

They may not have a use
we might not have enjoyed it
but they all had a part
because here we are.

## Zuzu Johnston (14)
Dollar Academy, Dollar

# Confidence To Make A Difference

Hiding away
cuddled up
full of opinions
not sure how to speak
anxiety coursing through me
and everything stops.

Stop
unable to think
my face goes pale
and the world feels real
my lack of confidence
stopping me from getting help.

Help
feeling vulnerable and wrong
insecurities
butterflies whizzing around
making me sweat
tears building up on my face.

Face
the way I smile
the way I speak

how I style my hair
how I laugh
concealing them only for me.

Me
a daughter
a sister
a student
a friend
a girl who has the confidence to make a difference.

## Freya Robins (14)
Dollar Academy, Dollar

# Future Possibilities

Holidays
The smell of the sea
Hot sun against your skin
New places
Pizza from Italy
Croissants from France
New friends
Funny and different
Almost like family
New routines
Waking up late
Getting a cup of coffee after work
New fashion
Big, bold dresses
Boring old suits
New houses
High-rise penthouses
Luxury poolhouses
New knowledge
Hobbies and sports
Uni and jobs

I'm excited to find out what I'm passionate about
What I love to do
And you should be too!

## Clara Gordon (13)
Dollar Academy, Dollar

# Past Me

No need to worry.
Please don't be sorry.
Life is going to be okay.

Life can be vile,
But don't put a pile.
Right on that smile,
It's going to be okay.

The sky is blue,
Get up and move,
Dance that worry away.

Stand for what you want,
Don't let others push and pull.
It will get better.
There is a light at the end of the tunnel,
You'll be there soon!

Soon the sun will shine,
And all will be fine.
Don't bat a blind eye
On how you feel.

**Ewan Macmillan (15)**
Dollar Academy, Dollar

# Current Affairs

Everyone should be in lockdown
For quite a while
And once COVID's gone
It will have been worthwhile.

The shortage of fuel
A worry in everyone's mind
Even though there is enough
And everything is fine.

Brexit has moved in the shadows
Completely unmended
It's the politicians to blame
And not to commend them.

There is a lot going on
Across the land
It's not all good
And it's mostly not planned.

**David Kelly (14)**
Dollar Academy, Dollar

# What Do You Stand For?

What makes you, you?
Your clothes, your height, your figure?
Where you live, who you know, what you look like?
Or is it what you stand for?

What do you stand for?

You might stand up against racism,
You might stand up for equality,
You might stand up for pride,

What do you stand for?

You might stand up against war,
You might stand for freedom,
You might stand for rights.

What do you stand for?

**Adam Hill (14)**
Dollar Academy, Dollar

# Dream

Dream big
Dream small
About anything at all
Dream about your future
Dream about your pets
You can be a teacher
You can be a vet
It doesn't matter if you're female
Or if you are male
Something like your gender
Shouldn't cause you to surrender
So, if you keep on dreaming and carry on believing
If you try hard enough, you'll end up succeeding.

## Amaris Charles (12)
Dollar Academy, Dollar

# Alive

Nothing exists anymore,
Words blast in my ears.

I'm lost
My thoughts now floating in my mind
Winding in and out of my body.

Quiet
For just a second,
Still nothing exists to me,
My eyes blur in a constant stare,
Now not seeing,
But imagining.

## Esther Lang (15)
Dollar Academy, Dollar

# I Am One

I am one

One of five

And this is how I survive

I am tempests, storms and shocking sky
Hidden beneath fog that clouds others' eyes.
Always silent, always quiet,
Always trying to tranquil this stubborn tyrant.
When he is wrong, he is right
To his torturous denial I wish to cry
That things have to change.
That his world of his won't always stay the same.

Your tyrannical reign is insane!

But survival doesn't come this way,
To survive I must numb my brain,

I survive as I close my eyes,

I quell my broiling tide,
As I decide...
I shall not shout, I shall not scream
Just with sealed lips and scowling eye

I will build a barrier between
His world,

And mine.

The amount of my concave words and silent threats will only
increase my wall in strength and depth
All held together by a cement of one part pain and three
parts fury

Between us now there needs to be enough quiet for me to
feel free
I need this space just to think
To work without this constant fight, you spark when you are
in my sight
But what that tyrant...
But what you never see is
I am a storm,
I am a shocking sky
I do hold the power of a tempest within my eye
But I don't want to set them free
I only want to live peacefully

But you cause my ears to ring when you say a single thing
You make my heart get tight in anticipation of a fight
You tip my mood when you walk in a room
You make my day when you walk away
You tease my patience
Day in, day out
You push me

Over and

Over

Why?

Why do you push me constantly?

I've lost count

All you're doing is pushing me out!

And you will push

And push

Until five

Becomes four

And then I and you won't be the same as before

And then I will un-numb my brain,
Then I will finally get away,
Then I will be seen,
Then I can scream,
Then I will believe

Even though that was not the fate
You wished for me...

## Emily Aldridge (15)
John O'Gaunt School, Hungerford

# Goodbye...

He said, "Goodbye but we will see each other again,"
As he wrapped his clothes in a cotton cloth,
I peered out of the window at parades of men,
In immaculate uniform off to fight.

He straightened his hat and my mother corrected him,
A nervous laugh - the only noise to hear.
The sun beaming down but the darkness made it dim,
As we realised, we may never meet again.

I shouted down as he said, "Look behind,"
I couldn't get downstairs in time
He was gone, never to return.
And I missed him.

The pain was suffocating me,
The thought of the unbearable engulfed me,
The pain was irremediable.

I ran into the kitchen to see him go,
But there was no hope.
I cried, I sobbed, I screamed.

But the postcard caught my attention.
His writing all curved and the ink new.
Through blurry eyes I could read it clear,
"Goodbye, we will see each other again."

**Naomi Fox-Shatford**
John O'Gaunt School, Hungerford

# Longing, Struggling, Questioning

Longing, struggling, questioning
Wanting, splurging, consuming.

They didn't have enough to buy some bread,
They always had enough to own and were widespread.
All their stomachs kept grumbling,
They enjoyed chucking a couple of grand to indulge in their gambling.

He didn't have a lot and his family said it was okay;
He worked day and night but just needed a little more pay - he was trying.
He had a lot and his family always looked like they were on display,
He had workers that laboured for their minimal pay while he and his family planned for their next vacay -
He was cruising.

His fingertips looked like diminished matches, feeble and discoloured,
She just needed enough for the electricity to not be banished.
Her fingertips looked like a royal descendant's, soft, gentle and always well-mannered,
Well looked after by the best in Beverly Hills and a common attendant.

The child loved their toys, sticks, an old tyre and their
imagination;
The stick was the tough leather handles of their motorbike
and the tyres were thick wheels
The child liked their toys, a toy electric car that could do
sweet tricks,
Cool Lego that could build a whole empire and many other
things along with their imagination.

We live in a world, yet we live in two.
Either born with a silver spoon or born having to make do.

I know, you know, we all know.
We can't control what happens in our lives but over time we
realise
We have a choice and can actually have a lot of control

Longing, struggling, questioning
Wanting, splurging, consuming.

## Abriana McDonald (16)
John O'Gaunt School, Hungerford

# How Could Society Let Us Live Like This?

How could society let us live like this?
Segregation and separation.
The identities of the many are hidden from the rest of
society.
Heat unevenly trembling down our sorrowful faces as our
hijabs peer beyond our vision.
Herds of us yelling,
Many of us screaming,
How could society let us live like this?

Power dominates our inferior character,
As the patriarchy rises, society falls beneath them.
Hope becomes diminished and violence is society's domain.
Our feeble minds become brainwashed by the superior.
Hearts break,
Minds become clouded from the discriminatory minds of the
hierarchy,
A sense of hope that one day the inexorable power that the
tyrants hold will become impermanent.
And the derogatory attitudes will become extinct.
Only those who could still feel contentment are those who
have nothing to live for.
How could society let us live like this?

The flavour of joy melts away.

The destruction of smiles grows stronger and the feeling of freedom is no more.

The rights of our people have become so diminutive that the existence of a well-lived reality is rare.

If only our lives weren't colluded with fear and a petal of peace could be re-envisioned by our minds

And that sadness is not the embodiment of our nature.

If only we could live the lie that we most desired.

How could society let us live like this?

## Amy Muscroft (16)
John O'Gaunt School, Hungerford

# Our Birds

Birds.
Graceful little things devoid of Earthly care
Who sing and set the sky alight
On wings so light they skim the air
Mind so clear when they take flight
Body so free to sail the blue abyss
But where I'm from, birds like these do not exist.

No.

Our birds don't get to know
How the breeze feels. Whether the sun sets fast or slow
Over the horizon. Our birds don't get to taste freedom.
Don't get to have a choice.
For we are all controlled by those who hunt for more.

Tethered with iron chains
Gripping onto our legs.
Greedy hands keep our feathered collars in a chokehold,
ever-tightening.
Beaks taped, cursed with a soundless scream.
They do not care for our cries. Our pleads.

Fledged wings clipped and coiled with wire
To confine us into flightless beings.
We are cramped into a cage and cannot pass the threshold.
Why can't we pass the threshold?

No.

Our birds don't get to see past that monocratic shadow
Which looms and daunts and threatens our very existence.
Our birds can't cry, or scream, or fly off into the sunset,
They can't sing and sail the blue abyss.
But can only remain in chains
And dream of a life where birds like those do exist.

## Bebe Thatcher (15)
John O'Gaunt School, Hungerford

# The Boring Colour

White is quite a boring colour
In my opinion,
So why is it such a dominating one
In amongst each other?

Those people believe we are all equal,
But some who aren't that boring colour?
Their stories may not get a sequel -
As if the last few pages have been ripped out
Unwillingly.

If you are in a different saturation,
You may not get to your aspired
Life destination.
All because
Of that boring colour.

If you're not that boring colour
You'll get treated like
A speck of dust in the universe.
Transparent.
Disregarded.
Invisible.
But that's all humanity is -
Right?

Just a speck of dust,
Compared to
Earth's oceans
And Jupiter's moons.

Like that piece of dust in your bedroom,
That you don't hesitate
To get rid of.
You never think of it ever again.

So why?
Why do some people get treated like royalty?
While others
Get hospitalised for being themselves; happy?

Whether they
Love someone,
Who shares the same body parts as them,
Or
They are not
The boring colour.

Why?
Because,
At the end of the day,
We are all the same -
A speck of dust
In the universe.

## Katie Griffiths (15)
John O'Gaunt School, Hungerford

# Games And Gambles

A society sundered by the wishes of the selfish few,
master strategists in this game of chess they play with
people's lives
where losing a piece means nothing to them
but destroys everything for someone else.
We're left flinging chips and gambling -
stakes much higher than a few lost bucks -
every time we make our voices heard,
grasping, gripping, grabbing onto every chance we get to
make them listen,
the cacophony and clamour of cries rising above, above,
above
the clack of the roulette that they've rigged to let them win.
And once we're sick of our pleadings falling on deaf ears
and our ire falling on blind eyes,
seas of flags and banners will flood the street -
the release of pent-up vehemence in people silenced for too
long -
the drab grey roads incarnadine with fury,
we'll march across the chequered board of city streets
until
their
castle

made
of
cards
will
fall.

## Victoria Jaworska (16)
John O'Gaunt School, Hungerford

# The Woman Upon The Throne

Simple violence, a little more, an uproar.
Disgust dominates their pitiful tones,
voicing their thoughts, her power, unjust.
The 'vision of disgrace',
in their eyes, her gender and her race.

She holds her head high,
as they want her beheaded.
She reigns with ethereal grace,
their voices, they scream, "She's a disgrace!"

A woman dares to sit on the throne?
Casually frowned upon, like shorts in winter.
A woman of colour?
Mistreated, undervalued and criticised.

If that were you,
would you be able to take it?
Resign from the throne?
Move aside and resort to suicide?
Wait for regicide?
Never mind.
Take that how you will.
If that were you,
hold your head up high.

Ruin those that refuse to stand by your side.
Gain a power they can't deny,
resolve your conflict in perfect strides.
Stand tall, refute the fall.

## Miles Morris (15)
John O'Gaunt School, Hungerford

# War

As they drilled deeper and deeper into Russian territory,
The soldiers began to grow weary.
Their numbers declined.
They starved.
And they died.
The Russians scorched the fields,
French troopers began to yield.
Napolean thought about retreating but
The voice in his head told him:
"Keep going, just a bit further.
You've already made it so far.
It would have all been for nothing
If you turned your back now."
His corps reached Moscow
When the first snow of winter fell.
He couldn't stay for long.
All the emperor needed to do was to get out.
The grand army waded through the thick snow,
Russian forces went in for the kill again and again and again.
Their numbers were now dwindling
When the final few French soldiers struggled across the border.
Over six thousand soldiers commenced the incursion.
Less than fifty thousand returned.

**Lewi Kyle-Jacobs**
John O'Gaunt School, Hungerford

# War

Ichor splashed onto the mud-caked field
As if wine had been bespattered onto the mourning earth
Smoke the colour of serrated slate and the body of a snake,
twisted itself into the skies
Choking the gods from above
Bloodshot eyes opened wide with sickly dread
Like a vermillion cesspool, its grotesque optic eyeballs
stared blankly with no mercy contained inside.

War
Weapons brandished like sticks of trepidation, aimed
towards the enemy
Leniency was refused, it was not an option
As it was defined as weakness
It was a death battle, a never-ending cry of war
The screams of demise filled the air, it was like music played
to the opponent's ears
It was like the song of expiry, goodbye and passing.

War
The culmination of people's lives.

**Madison Stephens (15)**
John O'Gaunt School, Hungerford

# Dear Future Me

Did you get everything you ever wanted in life?
Or did you get a basic 9-5 job?
Misery.
Are you still longing for more?
Or are you killed with content?
Triumph.
Have you experienced the greatest things in life?
Or did it get too much?
Suffocation.
Are you battling day-to-day life with the love of your life?
Or did they leave too?
Love.
Have you lost sight of who you are?
Or are you thriving?
Depression.
Were you taught to love?
Or are you still cautious with your heart?
Gleeful.
Are you currently creating the woman you want to be?
Or have you given up?
Static.
Have you had the chance to have the family you always
dreamed of?
Or did it not work out?
Yours sincerely,
Past you.

## Rebekah Standen (15)
John O'Gaunt School, Hungerford

# The Son Of Jupiter

*Why?*

The dead breeze whispered nothing
Silence echoed thin
The suffocating desolation
Strangled all that was within

*Why?*

Flying here up above
A crimson crater hanging high
Will the hungry men leave their vanity
Or take what they want from the sky?

*Why?*

Because in the end you'll always know,
These men will sink far down below
To a place far more barren than this
And see what they have is so very far from bliss

But in the end you'll always know

You're hollow
You're hollow.

**Ben Brown**
John O'Gaunt School, Hungerford

# No One

There was no one
No one to turn to for guidance
There was no one

Nobody could hear her
Her strangled screams
Drowned out by the echoing shouts of the crowd
Nobody could hear her

The girl was surrounded
Bodies packed tightly into the room
Shoulder to shoulder, scarcely any space to move
Claustrophobia gripped her lungs
The girl was surrounded
She could barely breathe
Uncertainty congested the air -
An anxious atmosphere suffocated the crowd
She could barely breathe

There was no one
No one to turn to for direction
There was no one.

**Helen Gray (16)**
John O'Gaunt School, Hungerford

# Empower Yourself!

Conflict, weakness, power
Darkness
Overwhelming
Developing
Strength, pain, shame
Have the strength
To rise from pain
Have the strength
To ignore the shame
Even if you cower, make sure you
Ignite your power
Loyalty, work, empowerment
Loyal like dog to man
Work like a man on a mission
The mission is empowerment
Empowerment from within
Projecting onwards to others
Mothers, lovers and even people
Out in the suburbs
Empower yourself!

**Max Wheeler (16)**
John O'Gaunt School, Hungerford

# Iron Lung

Freedom
The transcendent privilege has been revoked and cold steel
takes its place liberte egalite humanite have been forgotten
Now replaced with control, prejudice and cruelty
Will no one help?

Captivity
The new normal
Thick leather
Iron castings
Chains
Metal
All vices to hold her in place
To keep her silence
To stop spectators from interfering
To keep them in the stands
Is anyone watching?

**Enzo Scarlett (15)**
John O'Gaunt School, Hungerford

# War

Day and the night the rings of guns
Stunned the innocent man's ears like the beat of a drum

Sirens mimicked the screams of men
Warning people like mice
As death-dealing swooped in like eagles
Dropping bombs upon the soldiers

The soldiers were scattered
Scattered across the duplicitous shrapnel
Created by flock of bombers
Diving down in an unearthly despair
Of the wretched land.

## Archie Boswell-Pendleton (15)
John O'Gaunt School, Hungerford

# War

War
Is a conflict carried on by force of arms
Love
Is a conflict carried on by waves of hearts
And there is only one victor
We're a mess, you and I
But the truth is
You captivate me
In ways
No soul ever would
In ways
No soul ever could.

**Maude Williams**
John O'Gaunt School, Hungerford

# Waiting

I waited years, wanting to be accepted by society
Changing my life to fit the appeals of modern day
Changing my eating
The way I look
Just to seek the small amounts of approval and yet
The sun has risen and set
And yet nobody cares
Nobody ever notices
No one knows me
Just a person passing in people's life
Slowly moving through, watching their lives move by
Watching people smile, watching people be happy...
Waiting...
Waiting for someone to acknowledge me
But no one does
No one ever does.

## Loretta Clements (13)

King James' School, Almondbury

# Game Day

The wheeze of the whistle sounded as the game kicked off,
My adrenaline was pumping, heart thumping.
My tenacity levels were up to the max,
First man sprinted at me so I chopped him like an axe.
Each one tried to get through our unstoppable defence,
Ducking, weaving, dummy passing, each one we sensed.
On the last tackle they kicked the ball high,
I spiralled into touch, they all gave a sigh.

Play is started by forming a scrum,
Heads down, arms linked, which team will succumb?
The ball was fed in, the challenge began,
Both teams pushed like they were moving a van.
The ball popped out and it spun down the line,
The winger sprinted past the fullback, just in time.
It was the first try of the game, the parents did clap,
The whole team erupted and leapt onto his back.

The battle continued, it could go either way,
Each team were exhibiting an outstanding display.
Fatigue kicking in, we were running out of time,
They were applying the pressure but still our defence was
really sublime.
30 seconds remaining, the forwards created space,
Instinctively we went for a drop goal while running at a
pace.

It sailed straight between the sticks,
We won over our opponents who were as hard as bricks!
Instantaneously we went to shake their hands,
The game was over, we had amazed our fans.

## Eoin Morris (13)
King James' School, Almondbury

# A Votive In An Unjust World

Society sells beautiful lies, woven with false fantasies and plagiarised inconsistencies.
Emphasis on the 'beautiful'.
They sell you the definition of beauty in
Small pictures,
Small ads,
Small sizes.
They lie and lie, taking the world down a deep rabbit hole of dysmorphia
They've got us all fooled.
"Skip the food today to be beautiful tomorrow!"
Selling the idea that beauty can replace sorrows;
Deep down desires implanted from subliminal propaganda.
They sell the idea that beauty is empowerment;
That if you are beautiful then you could have the world on a glowing silver platter.
Selling us the ideology that if we are beautiful, today will be exceptionally better than yesterday.
But all the empty promises they flaunt and they brag?
They lead us all astray; lead their young into a spiral of mania and disarray.
Society sells small,
Sells beauty,
Society sells perfection without exception.

Small models,
Small clothing,
Small life.
Sells the idea that the size of your waist defines your beauty,
The idea that beauty is empowerment.
That you are not small,
You are not empowered;
You are ugly,
A waste of space...
Perhaps society is small?

## Lilli Walsh (14)
King James' School, Almondbury

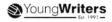

# Refugee

Miles walked
Family gone forever
Now in a camp in Calais
When will this pain go away?

I told the charities
I had a family in England
Will they let me in?
When will this pain go away?

I saw my twin die in front of me
Found my father's body
Saw my mum sink under the waves
When will this pain go away?

They are coming
Is this the day?
No, they've walked right past me
When will this pain go away?

The pain is still here
But I'm finally across the sea
Soon I shall be with family
When will this pain go away?

I'm in England
Still grieving

But I shall carry on for them
When will this pain go away?

I am now thirteen years old
Still the strange girl from Syria
The pain has finally gone
But I want it to return...

Please help everyone still stuck there
From when I was seven my life was hell
It's not their fault
Will you make their pain go away?

Just as others did with mine...

## Imogen Welsh (13)
King James' School, Almondbury

# Filtered, Fake, Cropped, Photoshopped

A perfect princess in a Barbie world
Is all I want to be
My skin flawless
Smoother than silk
Teeth that dazzle whiter than milk
Filtered, fake
Cropped, photoshopped.

Long blonde hair, glossy lips
Dress skimming slender hips
Thousands of likes adding up on the screen
What does all this false love really mean?
Filtered, fake
Cropped, photoshopped.

Strip away the filter
Peel back the layers
Look at what is really there
Skin is wrinkly, thighs touch
Anxious, self-conscious, worthless, weak
No filter there to conceal the shame
You can only find yourself to blame

Bodies change, looks fade
Life is about memories made
So ditch the filter, look up from the screen
See what life really means
Family, friends, happiness, laughter
Live your life a happy ever after.

## Lola Harber (14)
King James' School, Almondbury

# Winter

The sky is dark
The stars are bright
Nothing is cooler than this cold winter's night

There is nothing to be heard
Not a laugh, not a cry, not even a bird

Leaves are falling off the trees
In the midst of the gentle breeze

On the ground lies a white sheet of snow
Above the fence, the street lights still glow

The sky is dark
The stars are bright
Nothing is cooler than this cold winter's night.

## Chloe Taylor (13)
King James' School, Almondbury

# Chocolate Cake

Mmm... chocolate cake;
In my hand it starts to break.
Melts in my mouth as I chew,
My teeth are biting straight through.

A chocolate flake sits on the top,
It's something I wouldn't swap.
Harder and richer than the cake,
But it's a thing I couldn't make.

Chocolate buttercream oozes out,
I indulge the treat without a doubt.
Soft and creamy, sweet and dreamy,
It's so good I want to shout.

## Isla Farnsworth (14)
King James' School, Almondbury

# The Ocean

The ocean is a serene place
Where clouds would sit and melt
Peaceful is the world around us
Where rolling tides are felt

However, it is dangerous
As the waves wound the sands
But still I crept in the water
My life slipped through my hands

Icy-cold liquid slipped into my mouth
A sliver of muted fear blossomed in my chest
I knew instantly there was no way out
And eventually my mind was put to rest.

**Brooke Carroll (13)**
King James' School, Almondbury

# Green

The colour of nature
The colour of life
The colour of stems
That are picked off berries
The colour of grass
The colour of plants
The colour of the Earth
Before the days turn cold
Before summer becomes autumn
When the leaves dance down from the branches
When rain starts to pour down like tears,
Green, the colour of our Earth
That is slowly dying
The Earth that we are destroying!

## Hanan Lateef (13)
King James' School, Almondbury

# Breathless

Racism is not a trend.
So tell me, why did his life end?
He told you
'I can't breathe'
Which clearly you chose not to believe
He lost his life, that's in your hands
But clearly some don't understand
He wasn't a 'dangerous individual'
He wasn't 'resisting protocol'
In fact the only thing he wasn't doing was breathing.

## Kiana Beckley (13)
King James' School, Almondbury

# Hell's Orchestra

Do you hear that?
In blasphemous harmony, the woes of the victimised take centre stage
Hypnotised, the forsaken trash their skulls in a long-postponed rage,
With visceral melodies and barbaric screams, the relentless gutturals do tell
This is the language of retaliation, residing in the most crepuscular trench of hell,
I conceded with unapologetic glee,
This is the sound for me.

## Costya Whitehouse (13)
King James' School, Almondbury

# The Deciding Race

Cars zooming, engines booming - around the track they go,
Heading to first turn, dividing down the inside,
Turning round the corner with the podium in mind,
Foot slowly pushing down as the car accelerates,
Speeding down the straight as if they were late,
Crossing the line with the chequered flag waving,
In their history this memory is saving.

**Sam Fawcett (13)**
King James' School, Almondbury

# Power

Power
Powered
Empowerment
All things we should be careful of
Too much leads to jealousy
Too little leads to bullying
You have the right to have power
Everyone does
So don't go around bragging
Just live life how it is
You have power
Use it wisely.

## Eva Henman (13)
King James' School, Almondbury

# The Clock Ticks When The Time Goes On

Clocks tick when time goes on
But with you it seems to stop
Every hour and I wait for one more
Just to see you at my door
But as time goes on, you seem to go
You don't wanna see my face of sorrow
Clock ticks when time goes on
But for you I was just another one.

**Evie Taylor (13)**
King James' School, Almondbury

# Devotion To Your Flaws

In order to heal,
You must stay away from what hurt you
In order to move on
You must forget
But how could I forget you?
I'm left speechless
But I do have to say...
Devoting myself to you was the most reverting form of
dehumanisation possible.

## Georgia Lynch (13)
King James' School, Almondbury

# Winter

*A haiku*

Dark nights, seasons change
Snowflakes falling, my head spins
Swirling in the wind.

## Katie Shaw (13)
King James' School, Almondbury

# You Don't Have To Fit In

You don't have to fit in,
it doesn't matter if you're fat or thin.
Don't let others get you down,
stay positive and change that frown.
You are allowed to be emotional,
but it's hard when people aren't approachable.
Stay true to who you are,
just remember that you are a shining star.
Love your country and accept everyone,
not everyone has shoulder to cry on.
Never ever change yourself,
And I'll promise you will never be by yourself.
Stereotypes are a cruel, cruel thing,
don't believe them and get sucked in.
Take care of your physical and mental health,
go out for a walk and enjoy nature's wealth.
Look after our planet, we only get one,
If we wreck it entirely then all is done.
A leaf, a snowflake, none are the same,
we shouldn't be either and that is our aim.
Love yourself, you are beautiful,
You should never say otherwise because it is indisputable.
Be kind to all and respect their origin,
just remember: you don't have to fit in.

## Charlotte Reddington (12)
Loreto Grammar, Altrincham

# I'm Sorry

I'm sorry we left you with the chaos of this world,
I'm sorry we were too busy being dominated by technology,
That we forgot to do something because we were caught up
in our own doings,
I'm sorry we swapped our friends for phones.

I'm sorry we listened to people who defended themselves to
do nothing
We didn't notice how important the world was
We didn't know what we had until it was gone.

I'm sorry we were caught up in nothing
Until our own urgency became clearer,
As we realise we are nothing dearer than this floating body
we call home.
We know we're caught up in climate change,
But some say it will go away,
While some simple pray to survive another day.
I'm sorry, future generations,
I don't want to scare you but prepare you,
To dare you to dream a different reality despite disparities.
We all care to protect this world.

I'm sorry that we polluted the water and air,
I'm sorry we cut trees just for greed,

I'm sorry that we don't feel responsible for the planet we live on,
I'm sorry that most of us today don't even care about tomorrow.

Actually,
I'm not sorry,
Because an error does not become a mistake until you refuse to correct it,
It is up to us to take care of this planet,
It's our only home,
We are not apart from nature,
We are a part of nature.
To betray nature is to betray us,
To save nature is to save us.
If we don't all work together to save the environment,
We will all be equally extinct.

## Christelle Bitar (12)
Loreto Grammar, Altrincham

# To My Future Self

To My Future Self
I know you have been through a lot
Work through your pain
Everyone looks at you through distorted glass
Shatter that pane
No one knows who you truly are
Don't let them tell you
Be who you are
Be you, be unique
Pain may overwhelm you
Don't slow down
Full speed, go!
Wear a smile!

To My Future Self,
I hope you have achieved your dreams
To teach
Let out a joyous scream
You can do anything
I hope you helped people on the way
And gave them a smile
For your mistakes I know you will pay
Just keep going
I hope you enjoyed the trip

Have fun
Maybe take a flip
Enjoy!

To My Future Self,
Some memories may be beautiful and yet
What we find too painful
We choose to forget
So promise me one thing
Wherever you may roam
Remember the light
Guiding you home
Though the dark nights.

## Sophie Popplewell (12)
Loreto Grammar, Altrincham

# Identity

Identity
What is my identity?
What is my identity to those around me?
Hair, eyes, skin colour too.

What does my skin colour mean to you?
Black, white, brown or blue.
My skin shouldn't mean anything to you.

Eyes green, eyes blue,
Beautiful to those around you.
Brown eyes in the mirror, blue in the screen,
Hazel eyes in the ocean, staring back at me.

Straight, wavy, curly and powdered,
My hair is a way of talking to you.
Styled high, low or short just to show you.

Towns, villages
Cities, suburbs
Countries, continents
We all share the world -
That was made not just for me and you
but our opposites too

Meat, veggies
Supper to all the food,
Unknown to you

So don't discriminate
Or try to hate
Those that are different to you

Identity, identity
The thing that makes me, me
And you, you!

## Eloho Arorote (12)
Loreto Grammar, Altrincham

# I Believe...

I believe that you can achieve
Anything you put your mind to
Every day is a new day
Never let your dreams fade away
Everyone has different thoughts
Some in the past fought for what's right
Many have achieved great heights in their dreams
Be bold, be amazing, be you.

We are all different but we are magnificent
We all have different passions
Some might like fashion
If you are kind
You might find that others needed your happy energy
It's better than them being your enemy
The best thing in this world is you

Everyone should know who you are
You are the smartest person by far
You are like a shining star in a galaxy
Everyone is free to be who they want
Don't let anyone tell you that you can't
Life is too short to question your thoughts, so just go for it.

**Abigail Bailey (12)**
Loreto Grammar, Altrincham

# You Won't Know

Dear Younger Self,

How is the world?

You won't know, but soon a pandemic will happen.

When this happens you will see how truly beautiful the world is and what advantages you have.

You will talk more with your online friends and become closer.

You won't know, but there will be more pollution in the world.

Animals will die and the world will be in danger.

You need to help the world and stop this.

You won't know this, but you will be stuck at home for a long time.

Bored, bored, bored.

All you will have is the internet to contact people.

You won't know this, but the world will be endangered and forest fires will occur.

Animals will be endangered and sadness will devour the world.

So be ready...

The world might be okay at this current moment but you won't know what the future holds.

## Isabella Burton (12)
Loreto Grammar, Altrincham

# Stay Brave

To me eight years ago,
You may not know this yet
But some time soon
Grandpa will get
Dementia and he might forget
Your name and who you are

But stay brave
And don't be down
It may be very sad
Confide
In someone
And don't hide
It'll be easier to cope

You may not know this is yet
But in some year's time
The world will be hit by a terrifying large pandemic
People will get ill
You won't be at school
And time will be harder to fill
You may be worried
You may be scared
But stay brave
And don't be down
It may be very sad

Confide
In someone
And don't hide
It'll be easier to cope.

## Molly Kilburn (12)
Loreto Grammar, Altrincham

# Expectations

To the small person
To that small girl who believed that boys would always be stronger than her
To that girl who thought she must marry and care to be loved
To the girl who thought she must fit the mould of what they want to be liked
What they want, a carbon copy
To that girl
I'm still not perfect
I teach myself acceptance when positivity cannot be reached
I list what I'm content with about myself
Though the list is short, it grows
To the bigger person, to the woman who will find herself
To the woman who I hope grows into who I want to be
Make a change, be the difference
Love yourself if others don't
Be the stronger person
Only live to the expectations you set yourself.

## Alys Price-Jones (12)
Loreto Grammar, Altrincham

# Pretty

If the first word to describe someone is pretty
Then you must think twice
You're trying to be witty
Without paying the price

Beauty isn't what you see
Race or sexuality
Just let people feel free
To show their personality

Society tells us that the perfect women
Have perfect skin
Are not too fat
But not too thin
Have hair for miles
The perfect smile
Though they never look deep within

If all you see is someone pretty
Then you are the one I pity
As you cannot see the galaxies
Bursting from their souls
Limiting them to a specific mould
To a single word
Their voices still unheard.

## Alexandra Higginson (12)
Loreto Grammar, Altrincham

# Dear Future Me

Dear future me,
I'm writing from 2021,
I have so many questions like has World War III begun?
Has global warming stopped or are the sea levels still rising?
Although, to be honest, I guess that wouldn't be surprising.

Did the BLM movement succeed in a new, improved world sequel?
Is there no more homophobia and is everybody equal?
Is there no more homelessness or poverty?
Is there enough food for everyone to share?
Is there less war, more peace, more love and less despair?

So thank you, future me, I hope you see this letter,
And maybe you can tell me if the world really does get better.

**Amy Yates (13)**
Loreto Grammar, Altrincham

# Animals

We do not need to help them
it is ignorant to think
their lives are valued and they are worth something
it is estimated there are 16,306 species endangered
people say this needs to change
but this is ludicrous thinking
animal testing is necessary
and their lives need to be sacrificed for the good of mankind
it is a thought that
they take up much land
they are useless
they don't have feelings and emotions like we do
their lives are worthless.

*(Now read from the bottom to the top).*

## Cara Gregory (12)
Loreto Grammar, Altrincham

# Be Yourself

It's important to be yourself
As everyone else is taken, you are the only you
No one is the same, everyone is different
Everyone has different passions: sport, music art...
If you can't fit in, you were born to stand out
Make the change if something's wrong
Don't leave it
Make a change and change
Spread awareness of things you find important and things
the world needs to know
Nothing changes unless you mention it
Speak your truth and follow your gut.

## Elizabeth Stansfield (13)
Loreto Grammar, Altrincham

# Empowered By Mam

**E** vents planner
**M** akes delicious cookies
**P** lays Fortnite with me
**O** pens arms for cuddles
**W** ants the best for me
**E** arly bird that wakes me
**R** ests next to me
**E** ating pizza together
**D** iamond to treasure.

## Kian Searle (12)

Maesteg Comprehensive School, Maesteg

# Mum

**E** xcited by me
**M** arvellous mum
**P** owerful person
**O** verdose of energy
**W** orthy hero
**E** lectrifying conversation
**R** espected by others
**E** xcited by everything
**D** etermined to always take care of us.

## Tristian Bowen (12)
Maesteg Comprehensive School, Maesteg

# My Two Best Friends

**E** legant companions
**M** otivational sources
**P** ick me up when I'm sad
**O** nly two for me
**W** onderful to see
**E** xactly what I need
**R** eliable always
**E** xcited to play
**D** estined for me.

## Grace Finnemore (12)
Maesteg Comprehensive School, Maesteg

# Bestie Vibes

**E** very day always there
**M** y best friend
**P** artner in crime
**O** ne in a million
**W** orthy of time
**E** nergetic and uplifting
**R** espects me
**E** ndlessly empathic
**D** riving me forward.

## Daisy Purnell (12)
Maesteg Comprehensive School, Maesteg

# My Loving Family

**E** asy and understanding
**M** y biggest supporters
**P** eaceful people
**O** pen-minded
**W** illing to help
**E** mbracing always
**R** eady to listen
**E** xciting to be with
**D** ependable always.

## Linkon Edwards (12)
Maesteg Comprehensive School, Maesteg

# Around Alfie

**E** vening cuddles
**M** ood changer
**P** aws like parachutes
**O** beys my commands
**W** aits for me
**E** nthusiastic companion
**R** eady to go
**E** ncourages exercise
**D** oubts me never.

**Rhys Thomas (13)**
Maesteg Comprehensive School, Maesteg

# A Boy's Best Friend

**E** xcited to see me
**M** ucky like me
**P** layful puppy
**O** nly one for me
**W** agging tail
**E** ventful adventures
**R** unning free
**E** scape from reality
**D** on't ever leave me!

## Thomas Huggins (12)
Maesteg Comprehensive School, Maesteg

# Perfect Peter

**G** ood at fixing
**R** espectful to others
**A** nd
**N** ice to spend time with
**D** etermined to succeed
**A** wesome carer
**D** riven by love.

## Kyle Sparrow (12)
Maesteg Comprehensive School, Maesteg

# Empowered By Love

**O** utgoing friend
**L** ovely to be around
**I** ndividual and independent
**V** aluable soul
**I** mportant to me
**A** mazing companion.

## Logan Jones (12)
Maesteg Comprehensive School, Maesteg

# Time

If time had a name what would it be called?
If time could fight would it choose peace or war?
Flowers turn to poppies on these streets
Rarely people get out
But time won't stop moving
Her body froze when she heard her dad stopped moving
So I guess at some point I'm proving
Take value of the time that you're using
Head hot but heart cold
Feelings contrast, soul juxtaposed
It's hard to make a living on these roads
But if we ignore the misled and say no
The time will tell and the real will be exposed.

## Joshua Ogabi (15)
NWKAPS - The Rosemary Centre, Gravesend

# To My Past Self

Lots of decisions, lots of directions
Never easy, always precious
Time is consuming, time is effort
I gave up on life, all 'cause of my mother
Treated me like a child, which I deserved,
However, I felt like I was cursed,
I took it badly, I did the wrong things
Life takes a turn and truly begins
Now I've learnt my lesson
Family's important, these friends I keep distant
Life gets better but only if you try
Get help, better yourself
You'll get there if you try.

**Holly McAllister (15)**
NWKAPS - The Rosemary Centre, Gravesend

# This Is Me

When life gets tough you may get rough
Some days you may have to bluff
And tell people to get stuffed
Other days may be bright
And you can be a shining light
Remember to keep your dreams in sight

Children can be sad
But not always bad
They can make you mad
They may push and shove
But show them love
And they will fly like a dove.

## Riannha Samuel (15)
NWKAPS - The Rosemary Centre, Gravesend

# Lost

The world is a complicated place - I should know -
The trees grow, but why? The sea ripples, but why? The birds
sing, but why?
So many unanswered questions:
The answers lie deep down - hidden in the unknown -
Waiting to be unleashed, or so they try
Those answers scare me, I'm scared they will unravel truths
That will make the tears in my eyes fall down and cry.
Sometimes, people begin to feel alone - I should know -
Sometimes, your place in this world is hiding, waiting;
Waiting for the spark to start the fire,
Waiting for you to release the arrow from the bow.
Your heart begins to explore depths it's never reached
before,
Dreading, but not worrying about the cost.
The truth about everything is behind that closed door,
But when I finally feel the courage to open it, I feel more
once again lost.

## Emma Boddington (14)
Ryde School With Upper Chine, Ryde

# My Fellow Women

We enter the world as girls;
Our paths already chosen,
Our stories pre-planned and ready to be put into motion
We fight our ways through teenage years
Until we reach womanhood.

The catcalls and wolf whistles that ring in our ears
Remind us of all those tears
That we shed over men
That made us feel less than them;
Made us feel small, made us feel worthless.

They tell us our voices are too quiet to be heard,
Yet in the same breath we are told to not speak a single
word.
We're taught to be kind and patient to all,
But sometimes it feels like we are simply just walls
Surrounding a world designed for the needs of men.

To my fellow women... I say don't listen to them.

Layer together the experiences that shaped you
Together with the dreams that one day will come true
And pave your own path.
A path that is uniquely and wholly just for you,
And a story that is yet to be written.

Let no one tell you how to live your life,
And despite what feels like a constant strife
Stand strong and unite and be true to yourself.
Give a voice to the women who need it the most,
Keep fighting for the rights that we are so close
To achieving.

Be loud, be fierce, be brave and be free.
Be the woman that younger you always wanted to be.

## Alice Owen (14)
Ryde School With Upper Chine, Ryde

# Caitlin's Poem

She couldn't find herself,
Head always held high,
Skirt rolled up to her blazer,
Treating everyone like the dirt
Found on the soles of her shoes
Confident - arrogant even -
But the dead stare of her eyes;
Conflicting characteristics that confused us all,
Wondering, *who is she?*
When she didn't know the answer herself.

Who is she?
She no longer acts superior,
Skirt matching those around her,
Greeting everyone with a joyful smile and wave
As she treats everyone with the same respect
Even when she is treated like dirt.
She gets along with everyone,
But when she smiles - which is now most of the time -
The whole room beams with her,
Sharing the love of the person who took so long to be
found.

**Caitlin Dologhan (14)**
Ryde School With Upper Chine, Ryde

# Anorexia

You live in my head
You pretend to be my friend
I've listened to everything you've said
I just want this torture to end!

As I look in the mirror,
You make me scream with hate and I begin to cry
I tell you I'm still trying to get thinner
I trust you; you'd never lie

I can't eat food
I can't be fat again
But are you really helping my mood?
Just get out of my brain

I've been to hospital
People are worried about my weight
Is your voice really just little?
Why do you get to decide my fate?

This is my life to live
I've given all I can give
It's time to learn to be me
Anorexia, it's time for you to agree.

**Jessica Holt (14)**
Ryde School With Upper Chine, Ryde

# Imagine

Imagine the world we'd live in
if it wasn't for women like Pankhurst and Davison.
A world of segregation and hatred,
where women couldn't be doctors,
politicians, scientists or engineers.
Where women couldn't follow their dreams,
were forced into marriages,
forced into suppression
by those too small-minded to see
that this should never be a way to live.
And so, through inspiring women such as
Pankhurst and Davison,
women can get educated,
women can have an income of their own.

So be grateful for what these women did,
and I ask you,
imagine the world we'd live in
if it wasn't for women like Pankhurst and Davison.

## Catherine Brading-Palmer (14)
Ryde School With Upper Chine, Ryde

# To The Girl...

To the girl who hangs her head down low,
The one who feels even the pictures on the wall glare at her
as she walks slow,
The one whose heart shines so bright, yet is unseen,
The one who sits alone and lets her mind run free and
dream,
The one who desires someone's attention and kindness,
Yet she knows, she knows it's too overwhelming to
overcome loneliness,

The one whose stride became fiercer and taller,
The one who had energy and hope as she awaited her
caller,
The one whose mask unveiled the smile that spread across
her face,
The one who blossomed with confidence at her own pace,
To the girl who has her head held high.

## Cully Trevallion (14)
Ryde School With Upper Chine, Ryde

# Beauty Is The Beast

"Mirror, mirror on the wall, who is the fairest of them all?"
"Not you!" the tear-choked, filter-free face replies.
Phone filters: the false friends of a free fake reality.
Where parts are plumper and shadows erased.
Where black is blanked and beauty spots are no longer beautiful.
Which curve should be contoured? Which shade for my shadow?
Which nose is an up-do and which fringe is a fright?
Bad beauty bibles bulging with bulimic Barbie dolls
Beckoning us to be like them, look like them, smell like them...
But beauty coming from chemical-compacting companies
Is not beauty.
This beauty, is in fact, the beast.

## Ella Brear (14)
Ryde School With Upper Chine, Ryde

# Prayer Scratched Into The Telephone Mast

I know every teenager in the world says they're
misunderstood,
but I promise we're just looking for that serotonin,
for that goddamn instant validation.
We're native speakers of a language you don't understand.
The world outside is burning,
but we're just sitting in here, talking,
and still you say we're too young to be this sad,
we're just kids - we shouldn't feel this kind of bad,
but maybe coping can be religion if you do it right.
So I keep angel eyes in my pocket
and apple seeds under my tongue.
I wonder what will get me first:
the holy light or cyanide?

## Sophie Corry (15)
Ryde School With Upper Chine, Ryde

# The Only Way Is Up

They say the sky's the limit
But...
The open sky is so suffocating and
The ground supporting you is so useless.

You dream of something you
Do not understand yet.

So you tear at the sky
Dragging the clouds to rest at your feet -
Watching the sun rise and set for you
You unearth the ground you
Stand on 'til you can't
Find rock bottom
Until down is not an option.

Even when the dreams fade
And contort into nightmares
You know deep down that the sky
Was never the limit...
Because this is how stars are made.

**Finley Boxall (15)**
Ryde School With Upper Chine, Ryde

# 'Just A Scam'?

Every day I watch, learn and repeat
Things I don't understand.
I hang around different people
And change who I am.

I learn how to act,
What to say, what to do.
I stay quiet and watch
Just to learn what to do.

I change myself fully
Just to try and fit in.
But it doesn't seem to work
And I'm all lonely again.

I've acted for so long,
I don't know who I am.
Am I shy? Or confident?
Or am I 'just a scam'?

Cast all these thoughts away.
I'm happy with who I am.
Who I am, today.

## Wilona Rong (14)
Ryde School With Upper Chine, Ryde

# True To Yourself

When the clouds turn dark and stormy,
And you have no hope left inside,
Be you and no one else,
And no problems will arise.

Surround yourself with the things you love
And do them for as long as you can.
For if you stay true to yourself,
You'll be the best version of you that you can.

Let the golden sunshine fall upon your face,
Embrace the qualities that 'could be changed'
For if you can be your genuine self,
Life will be filled with happiness and grace.

### Alice Holyoake (14)

Ryde School With Upper Chine, Ryde

# Dear Girl

Dear girl -
be aware of this cruel world,
don't let its words get to your curls,
society is scared of dark -
it's your most beautiful mark.

Your skin is rich; it glows in the sun
don't let them hurt you, silence you
or make fun...
You are not the dirt but the
shining gold, bright and bold.

Tears of bleach will never light you,
brown and black - majestic horses galloping
in the beauty of the night.

## Aashima Maheshwari (14)
Ryde School With Upper Chine, Ryde

# Inconsequential

Inconsequential, the lie told to you,
This does not affect you, plays on rewind through your head,
Whilst judgement and sly smiles hide behind closed doors.

Inconsequential, mistakes make you better,
Mistakes they say are good, they say,
But mistakes lower your score, foretelling your
unforetellable fate
Of lies in the future.

Inconsequential. Inconsequential. Inconsequential.
Consequential to all.

**Kai Miller (14)**
Ryde School With Upper Chine, Ryde

# Habromania

The recognition in a familiar face
The acceptance of another
The likes of many
The hate from none
The resemblance to others
The influence from a heard person
All
Delusions of happiness.

**Lucie Dartigues (14)**
Ryde School With Upper Chine, Ryde

# Choice

What really annoys me
And makes me clench my fist
Out of all the irritating things in the world
This is on my list

When people ask me to decide
About this climate change mess
When really they should work it out
Instead of piling on the stress

They say we've only got eleven years left
So I don't know what to do
Please don't give me all this stress
It's your time to jump in. It's your cue.

In eleven years time
I'll only be twenty-two
So you see in eleven years time
There is not much I can do

And even if I did speak up
And really raised my voice
Nobody would listen
So don't dare ask me to make a choice!

## Evie Ellis (11)
Sir John Leman High School, Beccles

# If I Had The Power

If I had the power I would stop all wars
If I had the power I would save the world
If I had the power no animals would die
If I had the power I would help save the world.

When I have the power I will stop global warming
When I have the power I will make the world fun
When I have the power I will save the day
When I have the power no fights would be allowed.

But you have the power so please help us
But you have the power so please stop global warming
But you have the power so please make the world more fun
But you have the power so please save the world.

## Daniel Peckham (12)
Sir John Leman High School, Beccles

# Generosity

Superman flew around,
And then he discovered a boat,
He looked around until he found,
A peculiar disturbing sound,
He searched until he finally gave up,
Until his eyes fell upon a gold and silver cup,
He wanted to share it with the world,
But some need it more,
He flew and flew around until he came ashore,
He searched for a house,
Found a mother dying on the streets and heard her child
moan,
He said to the lady,
Empowerment is generosity,
Empowerment is authority,
Empowerment is a thing we all need.

**Samuel Thompson (11)**
Sir John Leman High School, Beccles

# The Summer Breeze

Summer once again struck the Earth
and Mother Nature properly awoke
all the flowers started to bloom
and the birds started their morning tune
I felt the summer breeze
when I saw the birds and the bees
I cannot wait for summer to properly start
when the sun is shining and all the clouds are gone
and when the summer fades away
I will pack my summer equipment for another day.

## Stephanie Roe (11)
Sir John Leman High School, Beccles

# Power

The world revolves around authority and power
Society tries to gain
Everything and anything that brings them a lot of fame

The world revolves around money and wealth
Everyone wants it too
They think it will affect them
They're foolish just like you

Power can make people insane
People try to fix it up
But have to try again.

**Benjamin Renicar (12)**
Sir John Leman High School, Beccles

# I'm Ready

When I feel low my confidence is small
I have almost none at all
But slowly I get stronger and stronger
My confidence getting bigger and bigger

I feel empowered and in control
I've almost conquered my challenges
I'm on top of the world
I'm ready for anything
Taking on my fears is just my thing.

## Xavi Lee (11)
Sir John Leman High School, Beccles

# The Power Of Empowerment

Power makes the world go around
Power drives people insane
Power corrupts the happiest of people
They try to escape but always in vain

Empowerment is the thing we need
Empowerment, everyone pleads
Empowerment will bring us salvation
Empowerment will clear the devastation.

## Hunter Renicar (12)
Sir John Leman High School, Beccles

# Faith Is Great

Faith is everything
Let us worship our king
God's the creator

He is powerful
He is strong
He is great

Look after this world
Get ready for the day
When all of us shall go to Heaven.

**Eden Benson-Smith (11)**
Sir John Leman High School, Beccles

# Empowered Or Not

You are the best
You are empowered
No, you're not
You are the worst
You are ugly
You are horrible
You are unkind
You can't do this.

*(Now read from the bottom up).*

## Kaila Smith (11)
Sir John Leman High School, Beccles

# You Can Do This!

*Haiku poetry*

I am sometimes sad
Sometimes I feel I can't win
But still I must try

You can do it all
You are stronger than you think
This is yours to win.

## Harry Thompson (11)
Sir John Leman High School, Beccles

# My Idol

A professional footballer by day
A youth fighter by night
Scoring goals
Sourcing meals
Champions League
Poverty food campaign
Fighting for the homeless
Fighting for poverty
Crowds cheering for him
On and off the field
Using his Man United status
To solve a child poverty crisis
Visiting homeless shelters, providing help for those in need
Recognising child poverty during a global pandemic
Fighting, shouting loud for those whose voices can be heard.

**Jamie Scullion (12)**
St Ronan's College, Lurgan

# COVID-19

The government told us it would be scary
The virus that would make us wary
Staying home is all we can do
We want to make sure our family is safe too
Thursday we clap our hands in honour
For the people who help our sisters and brothers
People make the masks seem such a fuss
But the vaccine will help protect us
Soon enough there were less smiles
And cases were rising by a mile
Social distancing means six feet apart
While trying to warm each other's hearts.

**Mia McDowell (15)**
St Ronan's College, Lurgan

# Dream Job

A new day and a new way
It's a new day and a new way
New things you will get to learn
New roads that will lead to a destination
Be prepared for this amazing ride
You will have to do many things
To make it the best possible time
You have that will to go beyond
You have the will to understand
So go beyond everything you know
Give your best shot in one go
All the best for your job
May you have an amazing time ahead!

## Enda Scullion (15)
St Ronan's College, Lurgan

# Why Culture Matters

Religious or not
Catholic, protestant, Muslim or Hindu
God created us to live, not start wars with each other!

Black, white, or not
It is a lack of disrespect to make fun of someone
Regardless of their skin tone!

Personality or not, we are all special in our own ways
Don't disrespect people's traits!

Overall please respect everyone,
Our cultures are special to each and every one of us.

**David Konon (12)**
St Ronan's College, Lurgan

# Why Is It So Lonely?

Why is it so lonely?
When my friends and family
Are by my side, they make me laugh
But why?
It's so lonely
When I sit on my bed
And wonder what it's like to feel
Someone's warmth but alone again
Depressed and miserable
But why?
Why so lonely?
Why so miserable?
When I can feel happy by myself
I don't understand
Why I can't feel free alone?
Just why so lonely.

**Ariana Pereira De Jesus (14)**
St Ronan's College, Lurgan

# Friends

We need our friends,
they help us become our true self
friends can come in different shapes and sizes.
As long as they are there for you
their appearance does not matter
friends help us with many things.
Such as, when you're feeling down
they can make you happy
and help you with hobbies.
Friends can always count on you,
and you can count on them.

**Ellie Towe (14)**
St Ronan's College, Lurgan

# Empowering Environment

Our world today
It's dying.
All thanks to us!
In years to come what will it be like?
Perhaps animals we love will be gone
Flowers and plants gone, all gone.
Maybe not as many trees, like forests.
How is the next generation going to live?
To save the planet we need to
Use less fossil fuels
We have to
Save our beautiful planet.

## Kaitlyn Farrell (14)
St Ronan's College, Lurgan

# Hairdressing

A job as a hairdresser can be difficult
especially when you do something wrong.
If it can't be fixed, you could possibly get fired,
but if you try your hardest it might never happen.

You can learn new styles,
and also new skills.
When you've learnt all the skills and styles,
you could start your own hairdresser's.

**Aliyah Armstrong (13)**
St Ronan's College, Lurgan

# Empower The Environment

The Earth needs your help
It's dying
We need to make changes in our lifestyle
Stop using non-reusable plastic
This ends up in the ocean
Start planting trees
This helps the Earth breathe
Stop wasting water
Start reducing, reusing and recycling
Save the Earth day by day
Together.

**Ava-Rose Keenan (15)**
St Ronan's College, Lurgan

# Image

It's hard to love your own body
with all the criticisms.
Comparing yourself to others
believing what people think.
Trying to reach standards
but they're set so high.
The feeling of jealousy
killing me slowly inside.

## Brea Lavery (13)
St Ronan's College, Lurgan

# School

School is important
School is fun
Cherish the memories you make when you're young
make sure to work hard and get good grades
Things may change and friendships may fade
So fulfil your potential and don't live in the shade.

**Ruairi Campbell (15)**
St Ronan's College, Lurgan

# Image

Asian, black, white
Nothing seems to be right
Gay, trans, bi
I want to cry
Why is our world like this?
I like someone but we can't even kiss
I hope this all turns around
Before we all have a big frown.

## Emma Mallon (13)

St Ronan's College, Lurgan

# Own It!

Love your body,
Feel empowered.
Own it!
Show off your imperfections,
They define who you are!
Why compare yourself to others?
Everyone is different,
Everybody is beautiful
And remember you look good.

**Sade Armstrong (14)**
St Ronan's College, Lurgan

# Summer Afternoon

In the sun
Having fun
With friends
Running fast with the sun at its highest
The fresh smell of green grass
I wish these days will last forever
Because the warm days
Are getting better and better.

**Dylan Jennings (13)**
St Ronan's College, Lurgan

# Forests

Forests are where
the animals can
breed!
But trees are all
gone because of
greed!
There must be something
that we can still do!
But do you still care
about the things around you?

**Connor Quinn (12)**
St Ronan's College, Lurgan

# The Environment

Trees swishing in the wind
Leaves falling to the ground
Animals slowly disappearing
Destroyed habitats to be found
The beaming sun
Melting ice.

## Olivia Crosby (13)
St Ronan's College, Lurgan

# Ghosts

Ghosts
They haunt you
And your dreams
The ones who say they don't believe
Are always the most afraid
They're always afraid of the dark.

**Beth Cushnahan (14)**
St Ronan's College, Lurgan

# My Dream

Beaming sun
Deep blue sea
Summer's sun
You with me
Feet in the sand
Ice cream dripping down my hand.

**Caoimhe Hatchell (14)**
St Ronan's College, Lurgan

 YoungWriters® Est. 1991

# YOUNG WRITERS INFORMATION

We hope you have enjoyed reading this book – and that you will continue to in the coming years.

If you're the parent or family member of an enthusiastic poet or story writer, do visit our website **www.youngwriters.co.uk/subscribe** and sign up to receive news, competitions, writing challenges and tips, activities and much, much more! There's lots to keep budding writers motivated!

If you would like to order further copies of this book, or any of our other titles, then please give us a call or order via your online account.

Young Writers
Remus House
Coltsfoot Drive
Peterborough
PE2 9BF
(01733) 890066
**info@youngwriters.co.uk**

Join in the conversation!
Tips, news, giveaways and much more!

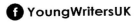 **YoungWritersUK**   **YoungWritersCW**  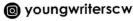 **youngwriterscw**